he said i was a peach

katie byford

For Lucy,

This little book contains foul
language, baby sharks,
broken bones & female wrath.
I hope something in it strikes a
chord with you!

[signature]

ignit**i**onpress

First published in 2021
by **ignition**press
Oxford Brookes Poetry Centre
Oxford Brookes University
OX3 0BP

© Katie Byford 2021

Cover design: Flora Hands, Carline Creative

A CIP record for this book is available
from the British Library

ISBN 978-1-7399058-0-4

Contents

standing close in the kitchen

teaching me how to tie knots in stems
with your teeth and my tongue

cheek cold and smooth as flesh
bitten, stones falling from lips
licked clean, glistening

dancing like two dangled
stems pinched in teeth

tumbling onto the kitchen floor, flushed

skipping into the heart of the house
the gem in its chest

our fingers staining all the doorframes red

Appetit

Persephone meets her betrothed

Bet is to be wedded than to brynne
he said I was a peach

couldn't see him didn't know the crocus
pollen on my toes would be a dowry

black earth gulped my legs my shoulders
covered my head my footprints with itself

the taste of aquifers stone forests
mantle *I am dead* I reasoned

through dusted lashes knelt
somewhere head bowed   informed I am

to be comfort for a mud king
with strange pets

I gripped a grass blade still
bright with my own kissed breath

there was a wed-ing of sorts
my stomach and other parts   surveyed

to fathom my capacity
hung from my feet to siphon sunlight

blood pressed for foxglove poisons
panned for gold molecules

then began the drinking   a feast of carrion
the maltworm king crowed his huge

knowledge of human weakness *how fitting you are mine*
he cracked   *for the price of your hunger*

how fitting he   the corpse lord   mistook silence
for surrender and half-sober stirs

face down on his throne mound   bound
under my foot my heel in grey cheekflesh

and at my word forfeits all but
everything of his   even the dogs

Still Life

After Dead Game *by Ferdinand Bol, 1646*

a wink through feathers

glinting flutter
   shuffled   slick

fit bird
        lucky girl
                    pinned up

  ankles in the air
        a varnish kiss
     brushed hand

       flushed
     with breath
stroke of luck
  plucked

            quick

glint of blood
     tethered

            bird   ankles
        pinned up   flushed

    wet splintered girl
        chick

   finger bone full house
        lucky hand

blushing   ruffled hair
        varnished slick

            kissed breath
                    spit

wings
                in the air
                        still

Swan Lake

Leda is seen by Zeus

his head is feathered

the lake of immortality
in his belly burning white

feet twist beneath him and his eyes
        black marbles in his face
                rolling wildly

                        both train on me
                        or the woman of me

picks me up with wings
can't tell which way the bed goes
        drops me on acrossways

                lets my skull dangle off
                        no face for now

neck parts fat with blood
something being offered

                the ancient heady taste
                        of something taken

and all the while I
am sober as skin

                as he the ballerino
                        steps forward
                        holds my frame in place
                and necessitates me

Honey

cellar of salt   mistook
for a castor of sugar
that ruined the baklava

just as carelessly   we admit
the stranger as he knocks
for that is the law

slip him fruit   from our pockets
bread and cheese undiluted wine
silent let him turn about the house his

finger-blistered wine glass   bread
crumbs butter knife door knob bannister
sticky footprints up the stairs

heavy boots thick   pollen
smeared on window
panes covered masked

reaching fevered hands   mouths
eyelids caked rubbed
amber sulphur honey gold

thick walls melt   waxen
between god thumbs
trapped beneath the ictus we

mourn in silence   robbed utterly
of every inch of our sweetness

Postcard from Aulis

Clytemnestra draws a bath for her husband

I'm cutting loose. It's not worth it.

I stay fast in the corner, eye fixed on a map
of the Greek resort, bunched up with the towels

and cigarette butts. No windows or aircon
but at least it's somewhere different.

You've been sunbathing with another girl
(Doris, or maybe Chloris), two sets of bleached
florescent teeth clicking together on the bathroom tiles

you shout at me *TURN THE TAP ON—*
NOT HOT ENOUGH   HOTTER   I unbutton my shirt
quietly. Chloris has a gull laugh. You fish up
lager and sand from your stomach
into the bowl, spit out a seashell. Resume snogging.

I thumb it idly then, this old note.
One corner inching out from my bikini top,

the size of a playing card, folded and folded.
The one you wrote me when

our daughter wasn't dead yet,
your big vowels smudged, nervous.

   DEAR TESS,
                    picture it - -
     a beach wedding for our little Girl !

         its <u>roasting</u> here
   we're sweating Daggers.   ~~drag~~dress her up pretty
        you'll see us at the Alter

       Party time !!

Some love letter.
Your puckered fingers choke the faucet.
Chloris pulls the plug, switches you off
—excuses herself to the lavatory.

I'm summoned and I come,
gaze lowered. I am your girl.

I rub sunscreen between your ribs.
I run the water hot and salt and beachy

and hold you under.

the angel & cash machine

feathers whisper and purr
inside the cash machine

on a sticky Soho of a Saturday
evening flecked with scattered kissing

strangers myself kissing a stranger who stares
drunkenly at my fingers feeling for my pin

number   she whips me into a frenXXy
with something like   *I only go for REAL girls*

not   you know   and stares at the other-
ed women peeling off into cabs the sting mixed

into the vodka on her breath she runs her fingers through
my long red unshorn locks never once guessing

that I am not always   *woman*   not entirely within
the body of that word sometimes this self demands

to be unsexed un-bilical an angel or celestial beast
that the   X   in my number cannot hold all this   denies me

credit   I tilt my head towards a Heaven of small flat
coins press my cheek against the silver gate lock my palm

in a kiss with the £100 button I have no right
to touch and remember I should never ask more

from a girl who believes I am   *girl*   and worth my
heft in gold and chromosomes breast and womb cunt and

lip copper hair   I beg change from the mistress who decides
I am a mistress and her   *no*   rings louder than pennies dropped

Mannequin

Galatea returns to her original form

He broke the surface of the water
with his hand to get at my hair

> *As you sink, light above moves in strange shapes*
> *tender dimples, melts to glass then mud*

grabbed at skin soaked through like cotton, milky
unvarnished eyes, lungs full up to the collarbone, solid

> *No time to forgive the cold: you curl inside it*
> *imagine yourself rapt in its coy smile*

porcelain teeth without lips. He dragged me feet first
dripping liquid, heaved onto the bank with a blunt *thud*

> *For the first time you appreciate the tongue*
> *terracotta baked helpless, cracked & split*

like marble crushes pillows, *Lakin* leaking swamp and silt
an object, full and empty. He drew close to touch his work

> *To be perfectly still is the only grace, you pray,*
> *that we are granted, that belongs to no one else*

convinced his lips, hands, some virility would
bruise me back to my old softness, my
self or at least a poem, before

> *You may feel nothing but the pressure*
> *at that depth will snuff you*

my brain was
a stone in
his lap.

Rearticulation

With a circular saw the nurse yawned
and cracked off the cast.
Inside, the foot, stuck back together,

looked smaller—*shrivelled?*
The nurse rolled her eyes. *Your foot,*
young lady, is the same size it was
before it broke.

I laid the new foot next to the old
for inspection, which took hours.
I measured and weighed each toe
against the other, just to be sure.

I ran a bath one metatarsal deep
for the newborn, dipped it in
and heard it take a faint breath,

wisps of dead skin sloughed off in my hands
to reveal a bald, skinny runt mewling
in the twinkling shallows.

Many evenings following
I cradled it in bed: *my glass bell,*
I would coo. *My squeaky nub of soap.*

I whispered it to sleep and nursed it
back to proper size. Its twin looked on
jealously, but lovingly, muttering over
and over *let this be our last repairing.*

artis

Arachne knows herself differently

are you spider silk? digit cling
and cling, winding sheet
for fingers quick and clean
suspended from your teeth, twisting

     shadow? hollow ground
       should have known   behind you
    stitched into your toes   warped
                       shuttle   blood

                you cobweb soon? splinter spun
          and dislocated tongue, wrinkled loom—

   will you fade then   weft thin
     softning

Fuck Salad

We both live with our parents, so we meet
in loud underground restaurants or *bistros*
for expensive food and shouted conversation

and talk nonsense about ex-lovers, how they kissed,
why we left: terrible men, wonderful women.
We order cheese, claw at the tablecloth. We should be

wrapped up in sheets, draped over ourselves
like sealions, smelling the other's hair
tangling with our own, half-breathing, but instead

we take turns describing the food we're eating.
The room's too bright to fill with poetry
or prayer, too dim to see the details of your face.

I can't spoon you, brush your hair across the table
over the bread basket. I can lick your knife
and nothing else. I'll cock my head

and, after some rough clattering silence,
offer you a bite of duck salad
that you're paying for anyway

or entreat a nip from a glass stained
with your lips, tilted gingerly
by gentle fingers into an open mouth

—a glimpse, quick rush of blood.
I guard the memory of that taste
in every nerve of me, saved like

a crumb under the table:
sanctified, sheltered behind the linen but
the meal foregone.

Son

Thetis remembers her mortal child Achilles

A diving bell with an unhinged head is the best treat.

Amid utter absence the bones glow. Elvers and shark pups
peck them dry. From that supper some are quenched
for an entire year, drag the floor with bellies full of tongue.

But they aren't the only hungry. The threshold of Hell
sinks further, colder. A filthy bed, one enormous dune
of undigested skin.

The oldest, smallest creatures take up in me.
I wake to their fond nips; I teem, create them in their need—
fill us up.

I call for currents, envoys set to burrow
into land, divide and eat it, to dissolve beaches,
pluck gables off their walls and swallow the contents
and bear it hence to many little mouths

        and yet. Your voice, I can
        hear your voice, a warm strain
      softening the frozen kelp, like piss

     mixed with grains from the sand that
     crusts your kneeskin.

  The message has formed a bubble;
  it drifts down, down to my seat
  in the dark, ringing with the wet
  clatter of knives and limbs.

You beg I come. Say it's urgent.
Please, Mum.

I sigh, draw myself back into a single body
defer the ocean's vast appetites

for this naked whelp, my finite child.

I rise in a pillar of silt, my chariot of anglerfish maidens.

Fine. Let us begin your second lesson.

EMDR Sessions

the light is silent
lone copepod   a pinprick in the dark

moves its single eye
back and forth
and I follow

sinking with it
into cold
memory or
dream

★

I am led
down and down in black
endless storeys

effaced in solid colour
no carbon body

no light
but the single
point drifting with me
bioluminescent

★

Where would you like us to begin?

the blue pearl rests on my eyelids
in the seaweed gathered about my neck

head circled in black ribbons

my filmy retinae full
       refracted I peer
             ahead

             below

                                    ★

I discover the first chamber
   flooded as you would expect

              wherever my
                 eyes go the glowing
                            nucleus follows

                            and wherever it goes I trace
                                tender details

                       I feel my body there
                       I hear my voice

            another voice

my
lids pinch
shut

        This room belongs only to you
             in every aspect

             look

             ★

further in I meet my golem
self again

        unspooling on the mattress
           eyes
             gaping

downwelling

           these are   facsimilia
               of histories
                   replicas in sand
                   and sulphur

        this time unclench
        your jaw

       ★

     in the room at the centre
of them all I am
five and a half

  cloaked in plankton

     my heart muscle the size of a satsuma

      brain still grappling with limbs and words

   infinite movement and noise

meandering over and over and over
    into the very first moment

        that I became a body

I am

so small
in this room

        ★

        cross-legged on the seabed

        I accept
      the first task

    in this moment
      lend her

  a fiction of
    power

    what does she do next?

Salt Creatures

We try at first to still the rush, the roar, but
as the swell reaches our chins we reconsider.
We will be sanded down, polished like seaglass
—the current rips and foams around us,

capricious. We boast burns shaped like open mouths,
blood-bright anemones on our necks, breasts; fingers swim.
I will drift with you over the ocean's edge
—our shoulders gleam, dolphin backs silver

and leaping. Held in an exhaled breath, small mercy,
our closeness carves a grotto between us, shivering with thunder.
You are a salt creature, let your spine dissolve
—we curl up in a periwinkle.

It dawns. You ebb and unravel, leave me clutching at
cloudy handfuls of sand, that curdle in the air as I retrieve them.
You will hear my breath in every murex shell
—the sea cave in me roars, cracks—opens.

Notes

The title of 'Appetit' is taken from the 'Prologue' to Geoffrey Chaucer's *The Wife of Bath's Tale*, as is the poem's first line (line 58 of Chaucer), which is itself taken from the Bible, 1 Corinthians 7: 'But if they cannot contain, let them marry: for it is better to marry than to burn'. In both texts, this is a pun on the heat of desire and the fiery demise in Hell inflicted for sexual intercourse out of wedlock.

In 'Mannequin', *Lakin* means 'little lady' in Elizabethan English. Possibly an abbreviation of *ladykin*, it is often used in the oath *by our Lakin* in reference to the Virgin Mary (cf. Shakespeare's *The Tempest* III.iii.1). It has later come to mean *toy, plaything*.

The word *rearticulation* in the poem of the same name means the process of reconstructing part or all of a skeleton after the individual bones have been cleaned.

In the poem 'artis', the title comes from *ars, artis*, defined in the *Lewis & Short Latin Dictionary* as: 'practical skill [...] esp., skill in a special pursuit, a profession, business, art: music, poetry; [...] oratory; [...] Cunning, artifice, stratagem, trick, fraud, deceit.'

E.M.D.R. stands for 'Eye Movement Desensitisation and Reprocessing', a treatment for Post-Traumatic Stress Disorder, in which bilateral eye movement is used to revisit and recast memory.

Acknowledgements

Thank you to Nick Griffiths who used recordings of early versions of 'Swan Lake', 'Postcard from Aulis', 'Salt Creatures' and 'Fuck Salad' in his music. Grateful acknowledgement to Rebecca Nisco who set 'Swan Lake', 'Salt Creatures' and 'Mannequin' to music for performance at Royal College of Music, and many thanks to Catherine Hooper and Harry Grigg for facilitating this collaboration.

I would like to extend my heartfelt thanks to Fiona Benson for awarding 'Appetit' First Place in the Open category of the 2020 Oxford Brookes International Poetry Competition. 'Son' was shortlisted in the same competition.

Many thanks to the Barbican Young Poets initiative for unparalleled mentorship which changed the course of my life in poetry. Thank you to The Writing Squad, whose workshops and support made much of this work possible. Thank you to Jacob Sam-La Rose for providing generous and thoughtful guidance on these poems. Thank you to Sarah Fletcher for her words of wisdom on early versions of 'Swan Lake' and 'artis'. Many thanks to Arthur Freeman for reading this manuscript. Thank you to Kym Deyn, Helen Bowell, Ana Sampson, Jack Selby and Lewis Buxton for their feedback, advice and friendship.

Thanks to the Classics department at Durham University, whose brilliant staff and students set me on this linguistic and mythic journey. Special thanks to Dr Sarah Miles, whose first-year module prompted the writing of 'Mannequin' and who has cheered me on ever since.

Thank you to my family for their love and patience, for wise words at the right moments. To Mark, for more than words can realise.

Grateful thanks to the **ignition**press team, and especially to my editor Niall Munro, whose insight profoundly shaped this pamphlet.